Genetics

From DNA to Designer Dogs

By Kathleen Simpson
Dr. Sarah Tishkoff, Consultan

D1337693

NATIONAL
GEOGRAPHIC
Washington, D.C.

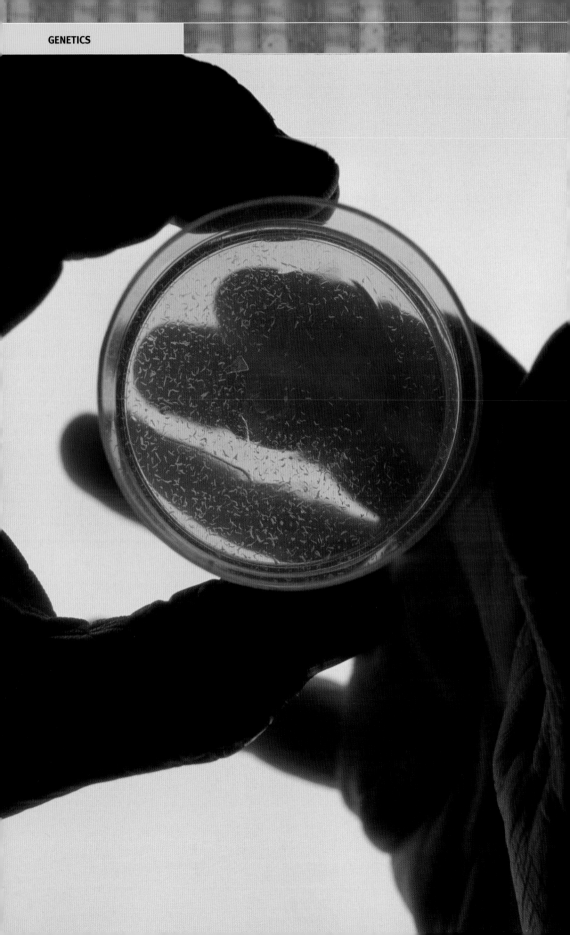

Contents

1   Ancient DNA   12

Royal genes • Pharaoh gone missing • Historic discoveries • A mysterious mummy is found • Family tree, written in DNA • Problems with ancient DNA • Genetic science reveals the future as well as the past

2   Genetic Science   20

Green pollution fighters • Rabbit genes in trees • Slow cleanup in the most polluted places • A medium pizza with genetically modified canola oil • A problem or a solution?

3   Genes for Long Life   26

Very old worms • Why is my hair brown? • Switching genes on and off • Inherited traits • Two points of view

4   Fighting for Wildlife   32

Mysterious animal on the loose in Montana • Gathering gorilla DNA • Extracting DNA • New weapons • Meet a DNA investigator

< A *Caenorhabditis elegans* worm in a petri dish. The worm is ideal for genetic research because it is almost transparent, allowing scientists to more easily study its internal organs.

< The mice on the middle and bottom layer of this tower were cloned from the animal on the top.

I first became interested in genetic research when I was an undergraduate student studying Anthropology at U.C. Berkeley. I wanted to use new scientific approaches to better understand questions such as, "When and where did modern humans evolve?" "What is the genetic basis of variable human traits such as height, skin color, and eye color?" In order to address these and other questions, I use anthropology, genetics, molecular biology, evolutionary biology, and computational biology. When I was a graduate student at Yale, I first discovered how much genetic diversity there is within and between African populations compared to populations from other regions in the world. This sparked my interest in studying African genetic diversity. For that reason, I have led research expeditions to Africa to collect DNA samples from thousands of individuals. From these samples, we have learned many interesting things about human evolution and African population history.

If you're reading this book, you must be intrigued by genetics, too. Perhaps your interest in the field will lead you to a career as rich and rewarding as mine has been so far.

Dr. Sarah Tishkoff
University of Pennsylvania

∧ Dr. Sarah Tishkoff (center) makes frequent trips to Africa, where she does research.

Mendel, the Father of Modern Genetics

Mendel studied seven different traits in pea plants in order to understand how those traits are passed on from one generation to the next, or inherited:

1) flower color - purple or white

2) flower position - axial (side) or terminal (end)

3) stem length - long or short

4) seed shape - smooth or wrinkled

5) seed color - yellow or green

6) pod shape - inflated (puffy) or pinched (shrunken)

7) pod color - green or yellow

Trained in mathematics, Mendel learned how to design experiments and analyze information. His studies of garden peas lasted 8 years, and he observed more than 25,000 plants! The conclusions Mendel reached about the principles of heredity in plants apply to people and animals as well. The way heredity works is basically the same for all complex life forms. (For more about Mendel, see page 15.)

< **1850 – 1860s**
Gregor Mendel investigates inherited traits in pea plants.

V 1953 · James Watson (left) and Francis Crick stand next to their model of a DNA molecule.

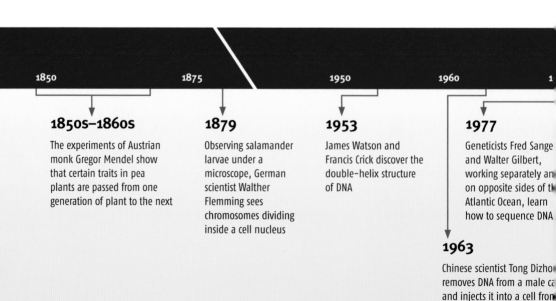

Λ 1879 · Observations of salamander eggs lead to the discovery of chromosomes, the biological structures where genes are located.

| 1850 | 1875 | 1950 | 1960 | 1 |

1850s–1860s

The experiments of Austrian monk Gregor Mendel show that certain traits in pea plants are passed from one generation of plant to the next

1879

Observing salamander larvae under a microscope, German scientist Walther Flemming sees chromosomes dividing inside a cell nucleus

1953

James Watson and Francis Crick discover the double-helix structure of DNA

1977

Geneticists Fred Sange and Walter Gilbert, working separately an on opposite sides of th Atlantic Ocean, learn how to sequence DNA

1963

Chinese scientist Tong Dizho removes DNA from a male ca and injects it into a cell from female carp, creating the firs clone of a vertebrate anima

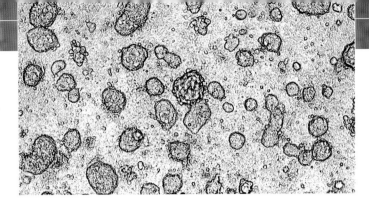

> **1998** · Embryonic stem cells hold great promise for treating and curing diseases in the future.

∨ **1984** · British geneticist Alec Jeffreys

∨ **1994** · The Flavrsavr tomato is the first engineered food approved for commercial distribution.

1980   1990   2000

1990

Doctors take white blood cells from a four-year-old girl with a disease that makes her body unable to fight off infections. They insert healthy genes into the white blood cells and put them back in the girl's body. The treatment is a success—the first successful gene therapy on a person.

1984

Alec Jeffreys develops DNA fingerprinting techniques that will be used around the world to solve crimes, identify people, and study animals

1994

A genetically engineered tomato—the Flavrsavr—is sold to the public for the first time. Flavrsavrs were made to stay fresh longer, and so, taste better. The U.S. government announced the tomato was safe to eat, but in the end, it proved too expensive to grow and market. Flavrsavrs are no longer sold.

2005

Using new, computerized tools that sort and sequence DNA quickly and precisely, the National Geographic Society and IBM launch a massive project to use DNA to map the migration of humans over the last 60,000 years

1998

U.S. scientists isolate human embryonic stem cells and use them to grow heart, blood, and bone cells

11

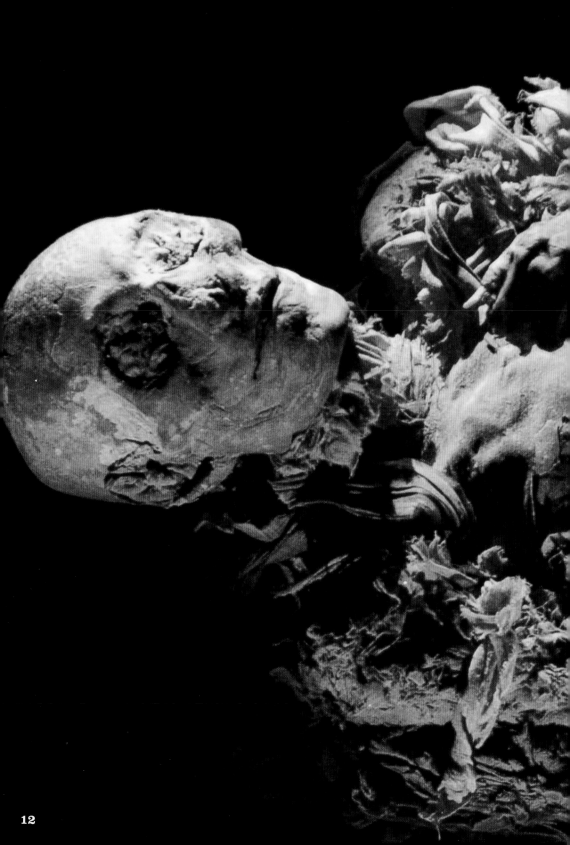

Ancient DNA

CHAPTER 1

Royal Genes

In the basement of the Egyptian Museum, a genetic researcher leans over an enormous female mummy. He observes the figure carefully. Dark skin stretches across the mummy's strong cheekbones and high, bald forehead. In the burial pose of ancient Egyptian noble and royal women, her arm lies folded across her chest, hand clenched in a tight fist, possibly to hold some sort of scepter, a staff symbolizing royal power.

The researcher works a long needle into the mummy's thigh, removing a sample of deoxyribonucleic acid (DNA) from her bone. The scientist then slips another needle into the same hole, but from a different angle, to collect another

< A photograph of the mummy of Queen Hatshepsut at the Egyptian Museum in Cairo, Egypt. The pharaoh's mummy was moved to Cairo from the Valley of the Kings in 2007, despite its first discovery in 1903.

sample. Researchers then whisk the 3,500-year-old tissue to the museum's new DNA laboratory, built for the sole purpose of studying ancient DNA. For their first major project, scientists are investigating whether the mummy is really Hatshepsut, Egypt's most powerful woman pharaoh—a king or queen of ancient Egypt.

Pharaoh Gone Missing

Hatshepsut was a queen of Egypt in the 15th century B.C. When her husband, the pharaoh, died, Hatshepsut's stepson, Thutmose III, became king. Thutmose III was only a boy at the time, so his stepmother acted as regent—a sort of substitute king. The plan was that when Thutmose III grew up, he would take charge, but Hatshepsut had other ideas. Declaring herself pharaoh, she ruled Egypt with an iron hand for the next 22 years. In order to make herself seem more powerful in a country dominated by men, Hatshepsut behaved like a man. She wore men's clothing, called herself by male titles, and even wore the false beard that male pharaohs wore.

When Hatshepsut died, someone ordered her image and name erased from Egyptian art and writing, and even her mummy was lost. Many experts think her vengeful stepson, Thutmose III, was behind Hatshepsut's disappearance from history.

▼ Archaeologists believe this is the lost mummy of Queen Hatshepsut, the 15th century B.C. pharaoh of Egypt.

Historic Discoveries

Modern genetic science is like an information volcano, exploding almost daily with new knowledge about the bodies of all living things. Early advances in genetic science happened more slowly.

An Austrian monk named Gregor Mendel (1822–1884) is often called the father of modern genetics. Working in the monastery garden, Mendel bred and crossbred thousands of pea plants and carefully recorded his experiments. He wanted to know how parent plants pass certain traits, like pod shape and flower color, to the next generation. He discovered predictable patterns in the way his pea plants inherited traits, and in 1866 he published his results for other scientists to read. At the time, few people paid attention to Mendel's experiments, but 30-some years later, around 1900, science rediscovered Mendel's work.

In 1908, a scientist named Thomas Hunt Morgan began breeding and studying fruit flies in his laboratory at Columbia University. In the famous "fly lab," Morgan and his students found that traits such as eye

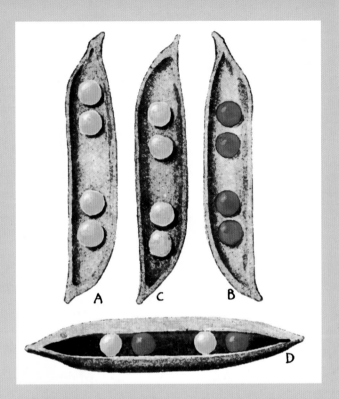

∧ A historical drawing of the peas used by Gregor Mendel in his experiments on heredity.

color are carried on specific chromosomes. The mother's chromosomes carry certain traits, while the father's chromosomes carry others. Morgan showed that genes line up on chromosomes, and their locations can be mapped. Today, genetic scientists still study Morgan's ideas about mapping the locations of genes.

In 1953, two scientists at England's University of Cambridge were trying to create three-dimensional cardboard models of DNA, the substance that seemed to determine how living things should grow and function. James Watson and Francis Crick knew they were close to discovering the structure of DNA, but their model was not quite right. Then Watson saw a vague x-ray image of DNA taken by a London scientist, Rosalind Franklin. The x-ray gave Watson's ideas a new direction, and he and Crick worked out the "double helix" (two spiral strands) structure of DNA. It was the biggest scientific discovery of the 20th century.

∧ The Valley of the Kings in Luxor, Egypt, was first excavated in the 18th century, and work on the tombs found there continues today. Many of Egypt's greatest rulers were entombed in the valley from the 16th to the 11th century B.C.

A Mysterious Mummy Is Found

In 1903, an English archaeologist named Howard Carter opened a tomb in Egypt that held two female mummies, one of them very large and posed like a member of a royal family. Because he was searching for a male pharaoh, Carter resealed the tomb with the mummies still inside. A few years later, the tomb was opened again and the smaller

> A monument of Queen Hatshepsut stands by her tomb in Luxor, Egypt.

mummy was removed, but the large mummy was left behind. Over time, people wondered who she might be: Was it possible that the woman left in the tomb was the missing pharaoh, Hatshepsut? In 1990, experts reopened the tomb to study the mummy, who wore a wooden mask of the type that might attach to a false beard.

Evidence began to pile up. Researchers found a wooden box in the tomb containing internal organs that they believed must have belonged to Hatshepsut. Ancient Egyptians believed that all parts of a dead ruler's body were sacred, so when hey removed a pharaoh's liver and ther organs during the process f mummification, they saved the rgans. A special box holding the rgans was placed in the tomb with he mummy. High-tech scanning quipment showed that the box ontaining Hatshepsut's organs lso held a tooth. When scientists canned the head of the large nummy, they found that she was nissing a tooth and that the hole n her jawbone exactly matched he tooth found in the box.

Experts announced that this mummy was the lost pharaoh Hatshepsut, and they set out to prove it with DNA.

▽ **An x-ray of the mummy of Queen Hatshepsut indicates where the pharaoh had lost a tooth while she was alive. The tooth was found buried in the tomb with her internal organs.**

▽ **Egypt's antiquities chief, Zahi Hawass, observes ιe mummy of Queen Hatshepsut (second, right) at ιe Egyptian Museum, where it is now undergoing NA testing.**

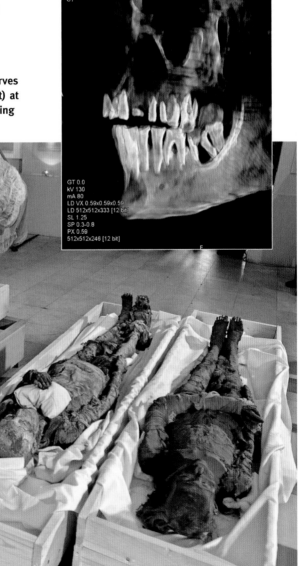

FELMALE KV 60 A FEMALE
HEAD 1 1.25 H80s
31490
Spirit
16-Nov-2006 03:49:43
CT

GT 0.0
kV 130
mA 80
LD VX 0.59x0.59x0.59
LD 512x512x333 [12 bit]
SL 1.25
SP 0.3-0.8
PX 0.59
512x512x246 [12 bit]

Family Tree, Written in DNA

Your body is made up of cells, and each cell has a nucleus. In the nucleus, there are 46 chromosomes— 23 from your mother and 23 from your father. These chromosomes are made up of a substance called DNA. DNA molecules are shaped like long spiral staircases, with a section of the staircase making up each gene. Genes carry instructions for how the body should grow, change, and work throughout its life.

Your family history can be traced through your DNA because you inherited genes from your parents and they inherited genes from their parents. Your DNA is similar to the DNA of your ancestors in very specific ways. In theory, Hatshepsut's DNA should show that she was related to other Egyptian royalty. In reality, proving anything with ancient DNA is complicated.

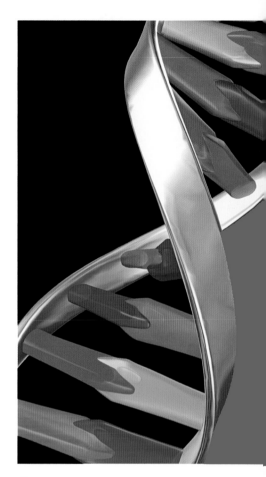

∧ A diagram of the structure of DNA

Problems With Ancient DNA

Ancient DNA is fragile, so scientists have a hard time finding samples that are complete enough to study. Another problem is purity; people who find and study mummies leave some of their own DNA behind when they examine a body. They leave fingerprints or pieces of hair on the site, and it can be confused with the ancient DNA. To solve this problem,

< Parents pass traits to their offspring through chromosomes, allowing researchers to map a family tree through DNA.

cientists take DNA from places where it is likely to be pure, such as inside a mummy's bone.

The large mummy's DNA will have stories to tell. Experts have already identified the mummy of Hatshepsut's grandmother and collected DNA from it. If the large mummy is Hatshepsut, her DNA should look a lot like DNA from her grandmother. Early tests seem to show that she probably is the lost pharaoh, but testing of ancient DNA can take years to complete.

Genetic Science Reveals the Future as Well as the Past

cientists now know that an ancient and mysterious universe exists inside tiny cells. In 2005, a *Tyrannosaurus* bone found in Montana yielded proteins (organic compounds) that may be 68 million years old. These proteins look a lot like strich proteins, offering strong evidence that dinosaurs are related to modern birds. In 2007, researchers studying Greenland's ice cap found bits of DNA that were between 400,000 and 800,000 years old. The DNA came from insects and trees, showing that Greenland was once quite warm, and changed scientists' ideas about climate history. What other secrets will genetic scientists find, locked up inside cells?

Almost daily, genetic science uncovers new information about the past, and it reveals a few things about the future as well. In years to come, genetics will bring new, better ways to clean up pollution. Chapter 2 describes how scientists use genes to grow pollution-eating plants. Chapter 3 explains the traits that children inherit from their parents and how people can use genetics to be healthier and live longer. Chapter 4 shows how scientists use DNA to save endangered species from an uncertain future, and Chapter 5 discusses microbial DNA and how microbes affect our planet. Chapter 6 explains how DNA and cloning are used in today's world. Exploration is an important part of what makes us human. What better place to begin than inside our own cells?

< Bones from a *Tyrannosaurus Rex* may hold clues to the creature's past.

Genetic Science

Green Pollution Fighters

In 1986, a nuclear power plant in Chernobyl, Ukraine, exploded and burned, spewing radioactive material across the Northern Hemisphere. Even as firefighters fought the blaze, radioactive particles settled out of the sky onto rooftops, trees, soil, and waterways.

In the weeks, months, and years to follow, radioactive pollution became a huge problem near Chernobyl. The area was evacuated. Cleanup crews chopped down contaminated trees and buried them in concrete pits along with cars and tractors. A thick layer of soil was scraped up and buried, too. Amid

< Sunflowers were used as a natural method of ridding radioactive poisons from the ground after a nuclear accident in Chernobyl, Ukraine.

∧ Sunflowers float on rafts in a pond less than a mile (1.3 km) from the Chernobyl nuclear power plant in 1996.

the racket of bulldozers and trucks, one cleanup project was surprisingly quiet: Sunflower plants were floated in ponds on rafts. The rafts had slats in them to allow the plants' roots to grow through the water. The plants drew up radioactive poisons through their roots. The sunflowers left pond water 95 percent cleaner than it was after the accident.

When governments tested nuclear weapons in the 1940s, scientists monitored plants in areas where nuclear explosions took place. They wanted to study the effects of radiation (a by-product of nuclear reactions) on plants, and to learn how long those effects would last in soil and groundwater. These early experiments proved that plants draw radioactive pollutants out of the ground. Then, in the 1990s, researchers became interested in using plants to clean up polluted environments.

At first, some people thought the idea was far-fetched, but now, experts rely on plants to clean up pollution, even at some of the world's most polluted sites. Plants do the job for less money than it would cost to scrape up acres of dirt and haul it to a toxic waste dump. They leave the area looking nicer, too, but there is one problem: Plants work very slowly.

∨ The water-cooling facility at the Chernobyl nuclear power plant in 1986. Fallout from an explosion at the plant contaminated many parts of Europe, the Soviet Union, and some areas of North America.

Rabbit Genes in Trees

Genetic scientists would like to make pollution-eating plants work faster. In laboratories at the University of Washington, Sharon Doty and her team may have found a way to do that. Dr. Doty takes genes from the livers of rabbits and inserts them into young poplar trees. All living things have genes that carry instructions for how cells should work. These instructions are different between animals and plants, but they are "written" in the same genetic code. So, in some cases, a plant can follow instructions from a mammal's gene. Both rabbits and poplar trees have genes that help them break down pollutants. Scientists already knew how to "turn up" the rabbit gene, to make it work faster. The transgenic trees (trees that scientists have genetically changed) eat pollution about 100 times faster than ordinary poplar trees do.

For now, Dr. Doty's trees are small, growing in glass jars in a laboratory. The team is looking for ways to alter the trees' own genes instead of adding genes from mammals. Doty thinks the trees will probably work even better that way. Researchers also want to make sure that the trees will not cause problems in the natural environment. Insects and other animals must be able to live in the trees and eat their bark, leaves, and roots without getting sick.

Slow Cleanup in the Most Polluted Places

∧ **Genetically altered trees are one way scientists are trying to combat pollution.**

The U.S. government lists more than 1,200 places as Superfund sites—locations that are dangerously polluted and need to be cleaned up. At the Aberdeen Proving Ground in Maryland, 30 years of testing military weapons left poisonous chemicals behind in the soil and water. In 1990, the government added Aberdeen to its Superfund list. The cleanup has involved scraping away polluted soil, removing old storage tanks, and hauling off waste that lay above ground. In 1996, the government planted poplar trees (the old-fashioned kind, not transgenic trees) to draw pollutants out of the ground. The poplars draw up about 20 gallons (76 l) of polluted water from the soil each day (think about the gallon of milk in your refrigerator and multiply that amount by 20). Even at that rate, this cleanup could take 30 years to finish.

Another problem is making sure the trees do not spread into natural forests. Some people see transgenic trees as a possible threat, because no one really knows what would happen if they spread. In fact, the U.S. government has strict rules about using transgenic plants outside of laboratories. One reason Dr. Doty's team works with poplars is that they grow fast, but do not flower for several years. This means they could do their work and be cut down before they produce seeds and spread. The team hopes to try out the trees in a few superpolluted environments.

A Medium Pizza With Genetically Modified Canola Oil

Insects can ruin a crop of corn. They burrow into the ears and stalks, feeding and tunneling until the corn is ruined, the leaves drop to the ground, and the stalks fall over in the wind. A whole season's worth of the farmer's work, time, and money is wasted. Genetic scientists wrestled with this problem and came up with an answer. They transferred genes from bacteria with natural insect-fighting abilities into the DNA of corn plants. The result was a corn plant that kills insects that feed on it, yet does not harm people who later eat the corn.

Since the 1990s, scientists have modified the genes in plants to suit the needs of people. Farmers have planted corn with built-in bug-killer, papayas that resist plant disease, and soybeans that are not harmed when a field is sprayed with weed-killer.

In the United States, genetically modified (GM) crops are so common that most people eat them every day in pizza, bread, cereal, or ice cream.

∧ **Insects known as corn borers can destroy entire crops. Geneticists have developed corn plants that poison the bugs that feed upon them.**

Most consumers do not even know when they are eating GM foods because they do not carry a label. For the most part, Americans do not eat fresh GM fruits and vegetables; instead, food manufacturers use GM crops to make packaged foods that consumers buy at the grocery store.

In the late 1990s, researchers developed a new strain of GM rice that was packed with vitamin A. They hoped the GM rice would help prevent blindness and other health problems caused by a lack of vitamin A. This could make a real difference in countries where rice is an important part of the people's diet.

A Problem or a Solution?

Around the globe, many experts worry about how GM crops will affect the environment. They fear that pollen from insect-killing crops will blow

nto nearby weeds, where butterflies nd other creatures might eat it and ie. They worry that the pollen from iM crops could be absorbed by weeds, reating "superweeds" that might take ver an ecosystem. Some people also ear that these new foods may contain llergens, substances that cause llergic reactions.

Other people look forward to a ay when genetically modified crops night solve many of the world's roblems. Will a poor farmer on a liver of land be able to grow enough iM food to feed a family? Will cancer atients fight their disease by eating itamin-packed GM foods? Will GM oods that stay fresh longer and ship

∧ **Much of Asia relies on rice to feed its citizens. Developing high-yield rice plants is one project geneticists are working on.**

easily allow consumers to eat more fruits and vegetables? Whether GM plants are a problem or a solution, they are already part of our lives.

∇ **Researchers grow genetically modified plants in their laboratories and hope the results they achieve anslate to large-scale farming.**

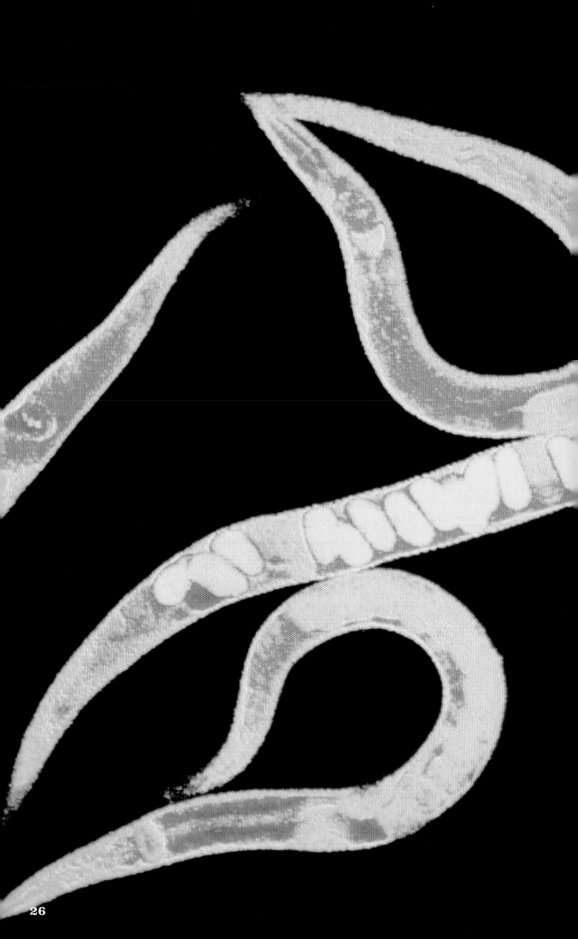

Genes for
Long Life

CHAPTER 3

Very Old Worms

At two weeks of age, a worm known as *Caenorhabditis elegans* lies near death, its body shriveled and barely moving. This tiny roundworm is a senior citizen, as roundworms go. *C. elegans* normally lives two or three weeks, and it shows its age just as most people do. Its skin changes, its movements slow, and it does not chase food with the same energy it had as a youngster.

Under a nearby microscope lies a cousin that is five weeks old. This *C. elegans* squirms like a kindergartner, even though it is more than twice as old as the other one. Scientists have found the key to long life in roundworms: Genes that keep

< Scientists study the DNA of roundworms for insight into aging and the genetic mechanisms that control it.

C. elegans young. Using chemicals and diet to turn some genes off and make others work harder, researchers have learned how to keep the worms healthy and strong, right into old age. Could genes do the same for you? Cynthia Kenyon, a scientist at the University of California in San Francisco, thinks it might be possible.

> A 103-year-old resident of Sardinia, Italy, still enjoys good health. Scientists look to people like her to understand whether long life is a result of genetics or the environment people live in, or both.

∧ Researchers study the short life span of dogs compared to the average human life span in order to understand which genes control how our bodies age.

For a long time, scientists believed that our bodies wear out as we grow older, like a machine with worn-out parts. Dr. Kenyon wondered why some animals live much longer than others. Why does a Labrador retriever live just 10 or 15 years while humans can live into their 80s and beyond? Could it be that genes tell the body how long it should live?

Why Is My Hair Brown?

Your genes determine whether you will have curly hair or straight, blue eyes or brown. Genes can even give you the ability to do things other people cannot, like wiggle your ears. These are inherited traits, traits you get from your mother, your father, or both.

Not all inherited traits are as obvious as hair and eye color, though. Genes can also influence the way you operate; athletic ability and musical talent are two examples. But this does not mean you can blame your parents if gym is the hardest class in your day or if you cannot sing like a rock star. Genes do not completely control your actions. Other factors, such as what foods you eat, where you live, and what you and your friends do for fun, also influence the ways your body's cells work. One of the trickiest jobs that genetic scientists have is figuring out how important genes are.

Λ Genes are not the only indication of an individual's potential for long life. A healthy lifestyle greatly influences how people will age.

Switching Genes On and Off

Each gene has its own job to do. Some genes control how people see colors, while others tell hair how to grow. Dr. Kenyon's team searched for genes that affected aging. They found one that made the worms live longer—twice as long, in fact. Then they found another gene that was a sort of "master switch" for several genes, turning them off and on. By experimenting with these genes, researchers soon had worms living five and six times as long as "wild" worms would. The old worms were healthy and active, wriggling under the microscope.

Inherited Traits

In Sardinia, an island in the Mediterranean Sea, a surprising number of residents are centenarians—people over a hundred years old. This is especially true among men. Scientists wonder why: Is the answer diet? A lifetime of hard work? Or does long life just "run in the family"? Scientists are still searching for answers to these questions.

You might be surprised at some traits that you can inherit from your parents:

■ Does your hair form a small point in the middle of your forehead? That point is called a widow's peak. Does your mother or father have a widow's peak?

■ Do you have a dimple, a small dent, in the center of your chin? Does anyone else in your family have a chin dimple?

■ Can you distinguish between red and green? Red/green color blindness is often an inherited trait, although it can have other causes.

■ Stick out your tongue and try to curl the sides of it upward. If you have brothers or sisters, see how many of them can do it.

■ Take a look at the back of your hand. Each finger has three segments, or parts. Does hair grow on the middle segment of your fingers?

■ Do the bottom of your earlobes attach directly to your head, or does the lobe hang free? What do your parents' earlobes look like?

∧ A Sardinian man, age 100. The high number of centenarians on this Italian island has led researchers to hypothesize that some people carry genes that code for a long life span.

Some of those genes that affect aging exist in human DNA, too, but it is quite a leap from tweaking the genes of a microscopic worm to extending the life of a human. Dr. Kenyon thinks science will make that leap, but only after years of hard work. Along the way, researchers may find other problems linked to genes. We already know that genes somehow influence many terrible diseases, including some types of cancer and mental illness. As scientists figure out which genes do what, they may be able to prevent some of the world's biggest health problems.

∧ **Dr. Cynthia Kenyon hopes scientists can apply the information they have learned from studying roundworms to study human aging and longevity.**

Two Points of View

If you could be strong and healthy at the age of 120, would you want to live that long? Some people say no—a life that long would be tiresome. Besides, if everyone lived more than a century, the world might become awfully crowded. Would we run out of food, water, and space for all those people? Genetic scientists argue that medicine has already helped people live longer than they did in the past. The world is already crowded, and these researchers think that humanity will adapt to future changes just as it has adapted to so many in the past. Why not live longer, they ask, if the body and mind are strong?

Crowds of people rush to work in Bombay, India, the fifth most populated city in the world. Overpopulation is an issue scientists who study genetics and aging must confront.

Fighting for Wildlife

CHAPTER 4

Mysterious Animal on the Loose in Montana

A large package sits on the desk of DNA investigator Dyan Straughan. The package is wrapped in the special tape that investigators use to seal packages containing evidence. Straughan knows what it contains. Newspapers and radios have covered the story for weeks: Some kind of animal had slaughtered 120 sheep on ranches across Montana. Witnesses had seen the beast, but no one was sure what it was—a wolf? a dog? Whatever it was, the animal cost ranchers a lot of money, so they called the Montana Department of Fish, Wildlife, and Parks for help.

< Wildlife forensic scientist Pepper Trail, with the National Fish and Wildlife Forensics Laboratory in Ashland, Oregon, catalogs bones of bald eagles to create a database of eagle wing bone dimensions for use in future wildlife crime cases.

∧ The pathology lab at the NFW Forensics Laboratory in Ashland, Oregon. Animal carcasses are laid out for study by scientists in order to identify the species.

The state then called the federal government, because federal law protects wolves. Federal agents, agreeing that the animal was a threat, finally found it and killed it, but they still were not sure what it was. So they sent its body to the National Fish and Wildlife Forensics Laboratory in Ashland, Oregon, where it ended up on Straughan's desk.

She opens the package and examines the carcass carefully. The animal's coloring is unusual—a little more yellow than is normal for a wolf. She uses a razor to slice off a tiny piece of its ear, about one-fourth the size of a pencil eraser. That tiny snippet of tissue will yield more than enough DNA to identify what type of animal killed the sheep. Genetic science is a powerful tool in the hands of investigators, helping them solve wildlife mysteries that would once have been unsolvable.

The Ashland laboratory, the most advanced wildlife forensics ab in the world, is dedicated to solving crimes against protected wildlife. Using DNA, investigators can tell exactly what species a sample comes from. They can, for example, analyze DNA from a shipment of leather shoes entering the country and compare it to the DNA of endangered caimans (a smaller cousin of an alligator). If the leather is made from the hide of a protected species, the shoes are confiscated and the seller pays a hefty fine. In a well-known Oregon case, investigators used DNA science to nab a merchant selling powder made from the horn of an endangered black rhinoceros. Most of the time, powders labeled as rhinoceros horn are really made from bones of other animals. By analyzing DNA in the powder, though, scientists learned that the Oregon merchant really did have in his shop a horn from a black rhinoceros. Just having the powder for sale is against the law.

Wildlife crime investigators can even link DNA evidence to a particular animal. When local residents report a possible poaching incident, investigators can analyze DNA samples collected from blood spots at the scene. They compare that DNA to meat found in a poacher's freezer or hides hanging on

∧ Boots covered in skins can be analyzed to determine whether they are made from the hides of protected species.

his wall. If both the sample and the meat or hide come from the same endangered antelope, the poacher may be arrested, tried, fined, or even jailed. Knowing that they could be punished may give some poachers second thoughts about killing protected wildlife.

> Wildlife forensic scientists are charged with determining if products are made out of species protected by law, including caimans.

Gathering Gorilla DNA

∧ **DNA fingerprinting helps researchers and conservationists protect the endangered lowland gorilla.**

Elbowing through thick underbrush, researchers in Gabon, a country in Africa, keep sharp eyes out for snags of gorilla hair on tree limbs or fallen logs. They scour the rain forest for hair, dung, and nesting places of western lowland gorillas, an endangered ape. The samples will yield DNA fingerprints of individual gorillas, telling the scientists where they gather, which ones move together, and how they die.

Finding and studying gorillas in the dense jungle is difficult, so researchers have never really understood how western lowland gorilla groups live. DNA science is changing all that.

When scientists found the carcass of a dead silverback (male gorilla) in 1993, they collected hairs from the scene. They could tell that the silverback had died in a fight with another gorilla, but they did not know which one killed it or why. Years later, they analyzed the hairs from the carcass, along with other hairs and dung collected in the area. Using DNA fingerprinting, they learned that another silverback had been nearby that day. They also learned that a female gorilla had left with the other male. Scientists concluded that the silverbacks probably fought over her and the female left with the victor.

This silverback was killed in a fight, but western lowland gorillas face other threats as well, including disease, poaching, and loss of habitat. With knowledge gained through DNA, scientists, governments, and conservation groups are working together to save the western lowland gorilla from extinction.

Extracting DNA

The first thing that DNA investigators do is find a usable tissue sample, such as blood, hide, hair, or bone. They dissolve the tissue and clean away anything that is not needed for testing, such as fat. Next, they do something called a PCR reaction to make copies of a section of DNA so that it is easier to examine. At this point, they may be able to identify the species, but not the particular animal. For that, investigators look for peculiarities in the DNA, chemical markers that are unique to one animal—a DNA fingerprint. To find out where the animal came from, they compare these results to the DNA of known groups, or populations, of animals in the same species. Scientists can consult animal DNA databases for mammals, birds, and other species to confirm their results.

▽ An image of a DNA fingerprint taken from an amplified section of DNA.

▽ A technician at the National Institutes of Health's Genomics Center works on DNA fingerprinting.

∧ Illegal wildlife products are seized by customs officials and made available to wildlife forensic scientists, who investigate the origin of the products in order to stop the illegal activity.

It can be a long, tedious job, because samples are often damaged or contaminated and do not always give reliable answers immediately. When this happens, the investigators keep working at it, sometimes for many months. A DNA fingerprint can provide a great deal of information—when investigators are able to decode it.

New Weapons

When Dyan Straughan finishes testing the mysterious animal's DNA, her results are a surprise. The creature's DNA shows it is related to three separate groups of wolves: a group in the Great Lakes region, a group in northern Canada and Alaska, and a third group that is found across North America. This combination would be almost unheard of in a wild wolf. Straughan concludes that the carcass in her lab probably belongs to a domesticated wolf or a wolf/dog hybrid, one that a breeder deliberately bred as a pet. The animal either ran away or was released, and it resorted to killing sheep in order to stay alive. The situation is a clear reminder that wild animals do not make good pets.

No pet owner has claimed the animal, possibly because the owner would have to pay for the dead livestock. Montana laws require owners of animals that are more than half wolf to register them with the state. They are also required to have wolf hybrids marked with a tattoo, but this animal has no tattoo and is not registered. No one is charged with a crime, but thanks to DNA science, the mystery has been solved.

Genetic science has changed the way criminal investigators and conservationists operate, bringing new weapons to the fight to save protected wildlife. Wildlife protection laws have been in place for a long time, but in the past, they were often difficult to enforce. Investigators relied on tire tracks, footprints, ballistics tests, and witnesses to link criminals to their crimes. These are all important tools, and investigators still use them today, but they are not always enough. Solid DNA evidence is often necessary to convict people who have committed crimes against wildlife.

Buying and selling products that come from protected wildlife has become a worldwide, billion-dollar business, despite the fact that it is illegal. In fact, illegal trade of horns, hide, and meat has seriously endangered some species. Wildlife forensics investigators like Dyan Straughan stay busy, searching for clues in animal DNA.

∧ Genetic fingerprinting has led to the identification of new species of wolves, in addition to helping experts solve crimes against protected species.

> This researcher works at the NFW Forensics Laboratory, the only crime lab in the world devoted to protecting animals.

Meet a DNA Investigator

Dyan Straughan is a DNA investigator at the National Fish and Wildlife Forensics Laboratory in Ashland, Oregon. Straughan works mostly on wolves. Any investigator can work on any type of animal, but by focusing on only a few species, each person becomes something of an expert on those animals.

▣ When people ask what kind of work you do, how do you describe your job?

▣ I work at the Animal Forensics Lab. The lab is just like a human crime lab, except that the victims are animals and not people. So if there is a poacher that kills a deer in a national park or a wildlife refuge, we can determine how it died—arrow, gunshot, poison—and match the gut pile found at the crime scene to a bloodstain on the suspect's knife and meat in the suspect's freezer. We do not answer questions like "does

this bird have West Nile [virus]" or "does this fish population have high levels of mercury." We only deal with crimes against animals, and, since we are a federal lab, we only deal with federal issues. We generally don't do poaching cases that deal with "out of season" issues or things like that. But, because we are a federal crime lab, we get cases from all across the country and the world. Since people often try to bring in animal products from other countries that are illegal, such as tiger products or primate products, those

items are sent to the lab for identification.

▣ What part of your work is most exciting?

▣ Sometimes, people will try to smuggle meat or animal products into the United States from other countries. People want to have things that may remind them of a trip that they took, like a necklace made from a lion's tooth or a bracelet made from the shell of a sea turtle. And sometimes people try to smuggle in meat to eat that reminds them of their homeland, things like rats, monkeys, or duikers a type of small African antelope). These cases are exciting for me. It's a real mystery to solve.

Q What animal [species] do you help [protect]?

A Unfortunately, all of the animals I work with have already died, so I can't save them.... I hope that the work that I do will help people understand that we (society) have rules about what is OK to kill and what is not, and we have those rules so that years from now, our grandchildren and great-grandchildren will be able to go and see elephants in Africa, lynx, wolves, polar bears, zebras, sea turtles, and all the other animals that each have their place in the circle of life.

Q What qualifications would I need in order to do the work you do?

A The minimum that one would need to do the work that I do is a bachelor's [degree] in biology. I have a master's degree in biology, with a focus in genetics. A Ph.D. is the best.

Q [That sounds like a lot of school.] Did you like school?

A For me, the biology was not that difficult, nor was the genetics (even the math was OK). I am HORRIBLE with language skills, you know, what is a prepositional phrase, what

∧ Mounted specimens of Asian gazelles are kept in the NFW laboratory so scientists can collect hair, horn, and tissue samples to compare to DNA they are investigating.

is the correct placement of a comma or an apostrophe. And if it weren't for spell checkers on computers, no one could even figure out what it is I am trying to say. Overall, I was a pretty good student, and I liked school....

Q Is there a "DNA myth" that you would like to dispel?

A You can't tell how old someone (or something) is with DNA—you start out with the same DNA sequence that you die with, age doesn't change it.

Q What changes do you expect to see in the field of genetics in your lifetime?

A I know that the methods that I use will be pretty old-school soon, but I do expect that we are well on the way to clearer understanding of the world around us, and that with the advances in technology, we can sequence the genomes of more and more species and use that information to figure out how processes in the cell and the body work.

Q Is there anything else you would like us to know?

A Even if you don't think that you will ever use science or math or physics when you grow up, really, it's not so bad, it can be fun.

Microbial DNA

CHAPTER 5

Why Is Microbial DNA Important?

In Yellowstone National Park, microbes thrive in water that stews at 150°F (66°C). Busily turning light into chemical energy, they grow in swirls of red, yellow, brown, and green. Could scientists learn to produce energy with the same efficiency that these microbes do?

In the polluted mud of Chesapeake Bay, other microbes "inhale" rust to produce energy, in the same way you breathe in oxygen to help you break down food to produce energy. In the process, the microbes change the rust to a solid form of iron that won't mix with water and is easy to remove. Scientists are investigating to see if the microbes

< **The DNA of microbes in hot springs at Yellowstone National Park in Wyoming is studied in an effort to learn more about energy production.**

can do the same thing with uranium. At a Colorado site where groundwater is polluted with uranium, the scientists feed the rust-breathing microbes, encouraging them to grow. The microbes flourish, and as they do, they change uranium to a solid form—one that won't mix with water.

Other microbes live around vents at the bottom of the ocean, where superheated chemicals leak into the sea. They live under pressure that would crush you, in darkness that would leave you confused, and eat hydrogen sulfide, a chemical that would poison you. They appear to have lived this way for billions of years, so scientists wonder if microbes like these can

∧ A technician works in a lab where thousands of strains of microbes are stored in deep-freeze refrigerators. Scientists are working on developing industrial products using living material rather than fossil fuels.

provide information about the beginnings of life on Earth. After all, microbes swarm all over the planet, outnumbering all other plants and animals combined.

∨ Samples of microbes are collected from the bottom of Great Salt Lake in Utah.

The 115-foot (35-m) *Weatherbird II* carries a plankton tow to collect samples for study in the Sargasso Sea off Bermuda.

Around the world, scientists want to know more about microbes—living organisms so small you cannot see them without a microscope. To understand how microbes do all the work that they do, scientists need to study their DNA.

A Map of Microbial DNA

Not long ago, the only method scientists had for studying microbes involved growing them in laboratories. Researchers grew one species at a time in glass dishes. If the microbe colony grew, they studied it under a microscope. But scientists also wanted to learn about species of microbes that refused to grow in laboratories.

In 2003, a team of scientists from the Institute for Biological Energy Alternatives (IBEA) and the Bermuda Biological Station for Research took a new approach: They scooped up water from the Sargasso Sea in the North Atlantic and studied everything in it. In this way, they learned about thousands of microbes in seawater and, more importantly, how all the microbes work together.

Scooping Up Life in the Sargasso Sea

The Sargasso Sea has long been considered a mysterious place. It is part of the Bermuda Triangle, where many ships have disappeared. Fifteenth-century sailors saw its broad mats of seaweed and were fooled into thinking that land was nearby. Even the wildlife there is mysterious: Young glass eels hatch and hide in the mats of seaweed, but no one has ever seen an adult eel there.

Unlike any other sea in the world, the Sargasso Sea is surrounded by powerful North Atlantic Ocean currents (bodies of water that move in a single, unified direction) instead of land. These

45

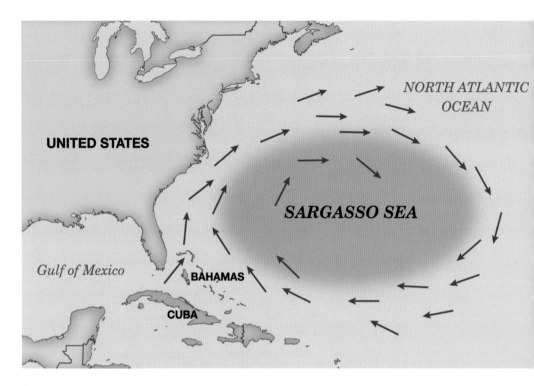

∧ The Sargasso Sea, in the North Atlantic Ocean, was long thought to be deserted of most organic life. Discoveries in 2007 showed that ocean currents bring nutrients to the region, allowing microscopic plants to thrive.

currents wrap around it like a belt, holding in the supersalty water. Scientists have studied the Sargasso Sea for decades, possibly more than any other part of the world's oceans. One reason the area was chosen for the 2003 study was that researchers expected to find a narrow range of microbe species. The water, they believed, held little food—not too many microbes for them to catalog in their experiments. It turns out they were wrong.

The IBEA researchers dredged up water samples from six research stations in the Sargasso Sea and poured the water through a series of paper filters. Each filter was

finer than the one before it, so that smaller and smaller microbes got stuck on the filter paper. The researchers froze the filters and shipped them to Maryland, where other team members used chemicals to clean everything off the paper except DNA from the captured microbes. Then they used high-powered computers and specialized equipment to break apart and sort out thousands of different types of microbial DNA. In the final stage of the project, they set out to make "maps" of the microbe genomes.

A genome is the hereditary information of a cell encoded in the DNA. Every species of plant, nimal, and microbe has its own unique genome. The human genome s different from the genome of giraffe, or a lemon tree, or a microbe. To map the microbe genomes, the IBEA team determined he nucleotide sequence of DNA.

Incredibly, the water of he Sargasso Sea was teeming with microbes. The researchers discovered DNA for 1,800 new species, including more than a million genes that had never been studied before.

Since the Sargasso Sea project, scientists have scrambled to learn more about microbial DNA. The IBEA researchers have begun a long-term project called the Sorcerer II Expedition to sample seawater in oceans around Earth. Traveling on he *Sorcerer II,* a sailboat equipped

∧ A crew member of the *Weatherbird II* hauls in water samples containing microbes for study.

as a research vessel, they take 53-gallon (200 l) samples every 200 miles (322 km). Just as they did on the first project, they strain their samples through paper filters, freeze them, and ship them to a U.S. laboratory, where another team studies the DNA.

∨ Scientists from the *Sorcerer II* Expedition take water samples from an inland stream in Mexico, looking for microbes they will filter out and freeze for further study.

The Human Genome Project

So what about your genome? How are you different from a microbe? For one thing, you are much more complicated. Your DNA is shaped like a tiny spiral staircase, with every step made up of two base chemicals. That staircase has about three billion steps! If the staircase was broken up into floors (first floor, second floor, etc.), each floor might represent a gene.

Human DNA has between 20,000 and 25,000 genes. We know this because thousands of scientists around the world worked together for 13 years, between 1990 and 2003, to make a record of human DNA. This huge project was called the Human Genome Project.

Your 20,000 genes are almost identical to those of other humans—very small differences make each person unique. By studying similarities and differences between people's genes, scientists are able to work out what individual genes do. It is an important task that will keep researchers busy for many years.

⋀ A bacterium housed inside cells in an insect has been shown to have the fewest number of genes in any known life-form, less than half of what scientists believed an organism needed to live.

Microbes live in the sea, in soil, in food, and inside the human body. People often think of microbes as troublesome "bugs" that invade the body and cause infection or disease, but that is not the whole story. Most microbes do not make people sick; in fact, their activity supports the air we breathe and the atmosphere that protects the planet. By studying microbial DNA, scientists hope to learn how to do things that microbes do naturally, like harvesting energy efficiently and removing poisons from soil and water. Microbe DNA may also provide new medicines and ways to manage carbon dioxide, a contributor to climate change. Because microbes have existed far longer than humans—about 3.8 billion years—they may even help scientists learn how life on Earth began.

Microbial Genome Project

Recent discoveries like the ones made by the IBEA researchers have piqued scientific curiosity about microbes. A massive project to research microbes, much like the Human Genome Project, has gotten underway—it is known as the Microbial Genome Project. With this project, scientists investigate not only individual microbes, but entire microbe communities. They want to know how individual genes help many species of microbes work together to solve problems, such as finding food in a polluted environment. Studies are being launched to investigate microbes in groundwater, in sewage, and even inside the human body. Early results show that microbes are far more important to humans than scientists once believed.

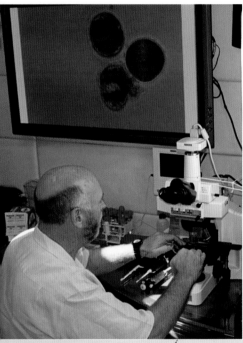

Dr. J. Craig Venter, a scientist aboard the *Sorcerer II,* peers through a microscope at microbes found in water samples.

∨ The *Sorcerer II* will circumnavigate the globe under sail to study microbial populations in both the sea and on land.

Genetics & Cloning

CHAPTER 6

Ditteaux, the African Wildcat

Ditteaux (pronounced ditto) looks a lot like an ordinary house cat. His coat is mostly gray with black stripes swirling across his back, and the fur of his belly is soft and white. Ditteaux may look tame, but, in fact, he is an endangered African wildcat. He lives in New Orleans, at the Audubon Center for Research of Endangered Species.

Ditteaux is also a clone. That means he is a genetic copy of his father, an African wildcat named Jazz. Scientists at the center think that cloning could be an important tool to use in saving some of Earth's most endangered animals.

< There is great hope that the endangered African wildcat population will be rescued by mating cloned male and female animals with each other.

How Does Cloning Work?

Here's how Ditteaux came to be. First, scientists took DNA from cells belonging to Jazz, an African wildcat that was born at the Audubon Center. Then they removed an egg cell from a female house cat. They took out the DNA from the egg's nucleus and substituted Jazz's DNA. Next, they applied a small amount of electricity to the nucleus, so the DNA would bond to it and divide, becoming an embryo (an embryo is the first stage of life). Finally, the scientists returned the cloned embryo to the house cat's body, where it grew into a kitten—a kitten with the DNA of an African wildcat.

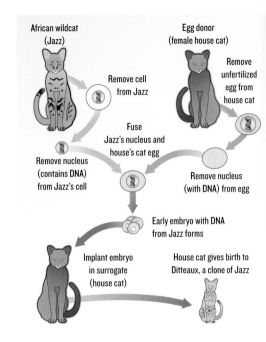

African wildcat (Jazz)

Egg donor (female house cat)

Remove cell from Jazz

Remove unfertilized egg from house cat

Fuse Jazz's nucleus and house's cat egg

Remove nucleus (contains DNA) from Jazz's cell

Remove nucleus (with DNA) from egg

Early embryo with DNA from Jazz forms

Implant embryo in surrogate (house cat)

House cat gives birth to Ditteaux, a clone of Jazz

∧ A cloned animal is the result of fusing cells from different specimens and embedding the resulting embryo in a surrogate.

Cloning History

Cloning is not a new idea; gardeners have been cloning plants for centuries. Every gardener who takes a cutting from a plant and shoves it into the ground to grow roots is creating a clone of the original plant. Cloning of animals is more complicated, but has been going on for five decades.

■ As early as 1952, a team of scientists in a Philadelphia laboratory cloned tadpoles.

■ In 1996, Scottish researchers cloned a sheep and named her Dolly, after country singer Dolly Parton.

■ In 1998, researchers in Honolulu used cloning methods to produce more than 50 mice that were genetically identical.

■ Noah, a cloned gaur, was born in 2001 in Massachusetts. Nearly extinct, the gaur, found in Asia, is much like an ox. Noah died before he was two days old, but his owners say his death had nothing to do with the fact that he was a clone.

■ In the 21st century, ranchers clone prize dairy cows, sheep, and other livestock. The process is expensive, so clones are used mainly for breeding.

Born in 2003, Ditteaux seems to be healthy, and behaves much like other African wildcats. In fact, he has fathered two sets of kittens whose mothers are also African wildcat clones (their DNA is different from Ditteaux's). The kittens themselves are not clones, but were conceived naturally. Dr. Betsy Dresser, director of the Audubon Center for Research of Endangered Species, seems excited about where this science could lead.

Problems of Diversity

One of the biggest problems facing endangered species involves a lack of genetic diversity. This means that most of the remaining animals in a species have genes that are too similar. Genetic problems are passed from one generation to the next, and spread throughout the species. When this happens, a species can suffer because of inherited weaknesses: a weak immune system or a genetic disease. Cheetahs are a good example.

At one time, cheetahs roamed over much of the planet—in North America, Asia, Europe, and Africa. Around ten thousand years ago, something happened to kill most of Earth's cheetahs—possibly fewer than ten survived. No one is certain what killed off the cheetahs (it may have been more than one event), but other species died out at about the same time, too.

Over time, though, cheetahs bred and gave birth, and the world's cheetah population grew. Scientists know this is true because of genetics; testing of cheetah

◄ Kittens born to African wildcat clones at the Audubon Center for Research of Endangered Species in New Orleans

∧ The cheetah population is at risk due to a lack of genetic diversity, making all cheetahs susceptible to the same health threats.

DNA shows that all the world's cheetahs come from a handful of distant ancestors. Genetically, they are all almost identical.

This means that they are all vulnerable to the same threats, such as disease or a change in habitat or climate. If one cheetah is affected by one of these threats, the whole species is likely to be affected. It is a dangerous situation for the world's cheetahs.

There is little scientists can do about the cheetahs' genetic problems, but they can try to make sure that other endangered species remain genetically diverse. For example, zoos can make sure that breeding animals are not related to each other. Governments can set aside areas for animal habitat, large enough to support genetically diverse groups of animals and plants. Cloning may become another part of the answer.

If an older animal of an endangered species lives in a zoo, an animal not closely related to wild populations, scientists can clone that animal. If the clone is allowed to breed with wild animals, the group becomes more genetically diverse. Here, though, is the really interesting part: Even if the animal in the zoo dies, scientists can freeze its DNA to use later.

Why Stop With African Wildcats?

In a dozen or so "frozen zoos" around the world, DNA from endangered animals sits on shelves in special freezers. Gorillas, antelopes, elephants, bears, and many other species are part of the collection. Scientists believe they can keep the DNA frozen indefinitely until, some day in the future, it can be used to save species that are dying out.

This does not mean you can stop worrying about the giant panda and the elephant. Some species are harder to clone than others, and for some, cloning may never be possible. Also, saving endangered animals will not do any good if they do not have the habitat they need, so it is important to preserve the animals' habitats, too.

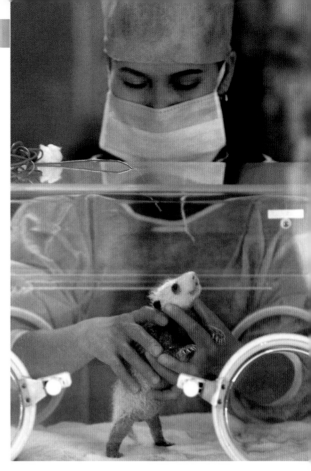

∧ A 16-day-old giant panda is held in its incubator at the Panda Breeding Research Base in Chengdu, China.

∨ A scientist at the Natural History Museum in London, England, observes a Polynesian tree snail. DNA from the snail and other endangered species will be frozen and preserved in an effort to safeguard the survival of animals that otherwise would be expected to go extinct within the next few decades.

Not all experts agree that cloning should be used this way. Some think that cloning science takes away money and time that should be spent on preserving animal habitats. Others point out that Ditteaux's embryo was carried in the body of a house cat. No one is completely certain of how the house cat's body may have affected the growing embryo. These experts caution that it is impossible to know what might happen if the DNA of clones like Ditteaux is mixed into wild populations.

Growing a Human Heart

Creation of human clones does not interest serious scientists, but the use of cloned embryos to grow human cells is another matter. Blood, brain, heart tissue—all these body parts can be injured or become sick, and scientists would like to know how to grow new cells to replace them.

∧ The Chinese government has unsuccessfully attempted to clone giant pandas. Scientists do not yet understand why some species are easier to clone than others.

Embryos contain a special type of cell known as embryonic stem cells. Most cells in the body have a specific job to do, but embryonic stem cells are different. They don't yet have specific jobs. These cells have the amazing ability to transform themselves into any type of cell in the body. They can grow into tissue for the heart, skin, or even brain. Not all stem cells come from embryos, though.

Take a look in the mirror. Right there, in the skin on your face, busy adult stem cells are already doing what scientists would like to do. They transform into new tissue to

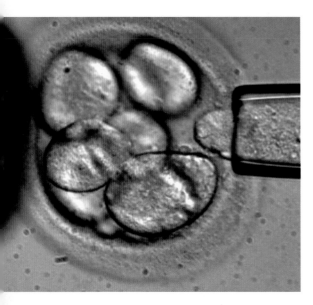

< A single cell is removed from a human embryo to be used in growing stem cells for scientific research. Stem cell research is a rapidly advancing field of genetic research.

replace the dead skin that flaked away last night in your sleep. In your brain, the same thing is happening, and in your heart, too; throughout many parts of your body, adult stem cells grow into new tissue to keep you going.

Adult stem cells are different from embryonic stem cells, though. Each adult stem cell seems to have its own list of jobs that it can do. Stem cells in skin transform into cells that the skin needs, stem cells in the brain transform into cells that the brain needs, and so on.

In 2007, something remarkable happened. Two teams of scientists, working in Japan and Wisconsin, announced that they had found genes that made adult stem cells in skin behave like embryonic stem cells. These cells were able to grow and change into other types of tissue.

Scientists have already learned how to slip stem cells out of the body, cause them to grow and reproduce, and make them transform into a different type of cell. The challenge now is to learn how to take stem cells from a sick or injured person, grow healthy new cells needed by that person's body, and then inject them into damaged tissue. There, these cells might do the work of rebuilding a weak heart or re-growing skin after a serious burn.

Scientists are still a long way from being able to grow body parts from stem cells, and some complicated problems stand in the way. The science is challenging enough, but questions about right and wrong may be even more difficult to answer. Many people feel it's wrong to experiment with embryonic stem cells, because embryos have to be destroyed in the process. These people feel that destroying an embryo means taking a life. Others argue that curing or preventing serious health threats like cancer and brain injury would save many, many lives.

⋀ Junying Yu, a scientist at the University of Wisconsin-Madison Primate Research Center and the Genome Center of Wisconsin, is a leading researcher in stem-cell technology.

The Years Ahead

∧ A Labradoodle named Wesley has a cream-colored coat like a Labrador that has the non-shedding characteristics of a poodle.

Genetic science sometimes moves in strange directions. The appeal of "designer dogs" is a perfect example. Dog breeders know that each breed has its own traits; for example, Labrador retrievers are playful and loving, and poodles do not shed hair. Breeders therefore crossbreed the two, hoping to produce a playful, loving dog that does not shed. But genetic scientists warn that the desirable traits do not always appear in the offspring. If they did, we would all be beautiful, intelligent, and talented.

Genetic scientists face difficult questions every time they collect a tissue sample, but these questions affect all of us. Where will genetic science take us, and how careful should we be about going there? What do you think?

Glossary

adaptation — random changes (mutations) in DNA that enable animals to survive longer and have more offspring in certain environments

adult stem cells — cells found throughout the body that are able to become one of a number of cell types

ancestors — people from whom a person is descended; parents, grandparents, great-grandparents, etc.

cell — the smallest unit of life

chromosome — the part of a cell that contains genes

circumnavigate — to proceed completely around

clone — a genetic copy

contaminate — to make something impure

DNA (deoxyribonucleic acid) — a chemical that carries genetic instructions for how the body should grow and function

DNA fingerprint — a description of the pattern of genes in a person or animal's DNA

ecosystem — a community of organisms and their environment that functions as an ecological unit

embryo — the earliest stage of development for a living animal

embryonic stem cells — cells found in an embryo that are able to become any cell type in the body

gene — a section of the DNA strand; a carrier of traits that may be inherited by offspring

gene therapy — the altering of genes in order to affect their function

genetic science — the study of hereditary characteristics

genetically modified crops — food plants whose genes have been changed by scientists

genome — a record, or map, of the order of all the chemicals that make up a strand of DNA for one species

habitat — the landscape and area that an animal or plant needs in order to live

hybrid — the offspring of two animals or plants of different breeds

mammal — an animal that is warm-blooded, gives birth to live offspring, produces milk to feed its young, and (usually) has hair

nucleus — the part of a cell that controls how it functions, sometimes known as the "brain" of the cell

organic — characteristic of living organisms

radioactive — giving off energy in the form of waves or particles that are harmful to humans

surrogate — a living host who conceives or carries an embryo

tissue — a group of cells locked together to form the structural material of a plant or animal

traits — characteristics

transgenic — carrying a gene that has been transferred from a different type of plant or animal

Bibliography

Books

Ridley, Matt. *Genome: The Autobiography of a Species in 23 Chapters*. New York: HarperCollins, 2000.

Articles

Kahn, Jennifer. *Mending Broken Hearts*. NATIONAL GEOGRAPHIC (February 2007): 40-65.

American Museum of Natural History. "Genomic Revolution." http://www.amnh.org/exhibitions/genomics/0_home/index.html (accessed May 22, 2008).

NATIONAL GEOGRAPHIC. "Food—How Altered?" May 2002. http://science.nationalgeographic.com/science/health-and-human-body/human-body/food-altered.html?nav=FEATURES (accessed May 22, 2008).

New Scientist. "Timeline: Genetics." September 4, 2006. http://www.newscientist.com/channel/life/genetics/dn9966-timeline-genetics.html;jsessionid=JAGIJHOIIFPN (accessed May 22, 2008).

PBS Nova. "Mummies 101." October 2000. http://www.pbs.org/wgbh/nova/chinamum/mummies101.html (accessed May 22, 2008).

On the Web

American Museum of Natural History
http://www.amnh.org/ology/genetics/

Audubon Nature Institute
http://www.auduboninstitute.org

Discovery Channel, "Secrets of a Lost Queen"
http://dsc.discovery.com/convergence/quest/lost-queen/program/program.html

National Geographic, "The Genographic Project"
https://www3.nationalgeographic.com/genographic/

National Geographic Kids, "Trapped in Amber"
http://www.nationalgeographic.com/ngkids/9609/amber/

PBS Nova, "Living at Extremes"
http://www.pbs.org/wgbh/nova/abyss/life/extremes.html

Thinkquest Gene School
http://library.thinkquest.org/28599/fundamentals.shtml

U.S. Fish and Wildlife Service
http://www.lab.fws.gov/

Further Reading

Double Helix: The Quest to Uncover the Structure of DNA (Science Quest). Washington, D.C.: National Geographic Society, 2006.

Genetics: A Living Blueprint. Minneapolis: Compass Point Books, 2006.

ndex

Boldface indicates illustrations.

About the Author

Kathleen Simpson lives in the hill country of central Texas with her two children, husband, and dogs. She has authored five books for young people. In addition to *National Geographic Investigates Genetics,* she has also written *National Geographic Investigates Extreme Weather* for the Society.

Consultant

Sarah Tishkoff did her undergraduate studies in Anthropology and Genetics at U.C. Berkeley. She received her Ph.D. in Human Genetics from Yale University in 1996 and did postdoctoral research in human population genetics at the University of the Witwatersrand in Johannesburg, South Africa, and at Pennsylvania State University from 1997 to 2000. She was an Assistant Professor of Biology at University of Maryland from 2000 to 2007 and is currently an Associate Professor of Genetics and Biology at the University of Pennsylvania. Dr. Tishkoff is a recipient of an NSF Sloan postdoctoral fellowship in Molecular Evolution as well as Burroughs Wellcome Fund and David and Lucile Packard Foundation career awards. Her laboratory studies patterns of genetic diversity in African populations, human evolutionary history, and the genetic basis of resistance to infectious disease.

∧ Triplets share the exact same DNA because they all originated from the same fertilized egg.

Founded in 1888, the National Geographic Society is one of the largest nonprofit scientific and educational organizations in the world. It reaches more than 285 million people worldwide each month through its official journal, NATIONAL GEOGRAPHIC, and its four other magazines; the National Geographic Channel; television documentaries; radio programs; films; books; videos and DVDs; maps; and interactive media. National Geographic has funded more than 8,000 scientific research projects and supports an education program combating geographic illiteracy.

For more information, please call 1-800-NGS LINE (647-5463) or write to the following address:

National Geographic Society
1145 17th Street N.W., Washington, D.C.
20036-4688 U.S.A.

Visit us online at
www.nationalgeographic.com/books

For librarians and teachers:
www.ngchildrensbooks.com

More for kids from National Geographic:
kids.nationalgeographic.com

For information about special discounts for bulk purchases, please contact National Geographic Books Special Sales: ngspecsales@ngs.org

For rights or permissions inquiries, please contact National Geographic Books Subsidiary Rights: ngbookrights@ngs.org

Library of Congress Cataloging-in-Publication Data available upon request

Hardcover ISBN: 978-1-4263-0361-6
Library ISBN: 978-1-4263-0327-2

Printed in China

Book design by Dan Banks, Project Design Company

Published by the National Geographic Society

John M. Fahey, Jr., *President and Chief Executive Officer;* Gilbert M. Grosvenor, *Chairman of the Board;* Tim T. Kelly, *President, Global Media Group;* John Q. Griffin, *President, Publishing;* Nina D. Hoffman, *Executive Vice President; President, Book Publishing Group*

Prepared by the Book Division

Nancy Laties Feresten, *Vice President, Editor in Chief, Children's Books;*
Bea Jackson, *Director of Design and Illustrations, Children's Books;*
Amy Shields, *Executive Editor, Series, Children's Books*

Staff for This Book

Virginia Ann Koeth, *Editor*
Jim Hiscott, *Art Director*
Lori Epstein, *Illustrations Editor*
Stuart Armstrong, *Graphics*
Lewis R. Bassford, *Production Manager*
Grace Hill, *Associate Managing Editor*
Jennifer A. Thornton, *Managing Editor*
R. Gary Colbert, *Production Director*
Susan Borke, *Legal and Business Affairs*

Manufacturing and Quality Management

Christopher A. Liedel, *Chief Financial Officer*
Phillip L. Schlosser, *Vice President*
Chris Brown, *Technical Director*
Nicole Elliott, *Manager*

Photo Credits

Front cover: Edinburgh, Scotland, 1996: Dolly became the first animal to be cloned from DNA taken from an adult animal.

Back cover: model of DNA

Page 1: A Labradoodle puppy exhibits traits of both Labradors and poodles. Scientists created a hybrid breed in order to isolate the most desirable characteristics of both breeds.

Pages 2–3: Fluid samples for DNA analysis are dropped into a sample tray with a tool called a multi-channel pipette.

A Creative Media Applications, Inc. Productio

Editor: Susan Madoff
Copy Editor: Laurie Lieb
Design and Production: Luís Leon and Fabia Wargin

Genetics

From DNA to Designer Dogs